CW01083895

This diary belongs to

____

The 2025 Irish Pages Literary Diary
is first published in hardback
on 1 October 2024.

The Irish Pages Press
129 Ormeau Road
Belfast BT7 1SH
Ireland

www.irishpages.org

Editors: Ciarán O'Rourke and Milena Williamson

Typeset in 12/14.5pt Monotype Perpetua.
Designed and composed by RV, Belfast. Printed by Bell & Bain, Glasgow.

A CIP catalogue record for this book
is available from The British Library.

ISBN: 978-1-7390902-1-0

The 2025 Irish Pages Literary Diary

Edited by
Ciarán O'Rourke
& Milena Williamson

THE IRISH PAGES PRESS
CLÓ AN MHÍL BHUÍ

FOREWORD FROM THE EDITORS

On Diaries

When I flip through my previous diaries, I find flight details, work deadlines, doctor's appointments, book launches, birthdays, drinks with friends, dinners with my partner and family video calls. I imagine that other people's diaries may be similar to mine, which is to say, *ordinary*.

Why keep a diary? And why look back at old diaries? The used diary has already served its purpose: it has shepherded us from that moment to this moment, from there to here. In *The Writing Life* Annie Dillard reminds us: "How we spend our days is, of course, how we spend our lives." Dillard's sentiment is shared by Emily Dickinson who, more than a hundred years ago, writes: "Forever – is composed of Nows –/ 'Tis not a different time – …" Keeping a diary, particularly a physical diary, gives a form to our days and lives, the forever (or whatever fragment of time we may have) composed of nows. My old diary – with its ink-stained cover, battered corners and cracked spine – is my body carrying me through the years. My current diary is the pleasure and the pain I have yet to feel.

On 29 December 2020, there is only one note in my diary: "Nothing with coffee." Normally, the days between Christmas and New Year's Day are a blur of family and friends, late nights and lazy mornings, blue winter light and long walks to familiar streets. Away from the office, we find that the time is finally our own. At this time of the year, the diary is often blank because the diary has not been opened.

In Belfast on 29 December 2020, however, an 8 pm curfew had just been implemented due to the Covid-19 pandemic. For me, making coffee, which I had only recently started drinking, was one of the few activities I could schedule reliably in my diary. As Zadie Smith says of writing, "It's something to do." In *Intimations*, she goes on to say, "Love is not something to do, but something to be experienced … that must be why it frightens so many of us and why we so often approach it indirectly. Here is this novel, made with love. Here is this banana bread, made with love." When I look back at my 2020 diary and read "Nothing with coffee", I am grateful that I could pour a cup for my partner and my best friend (also my housemate at the time), two people I still deeply care about today.

As I write this, I don't know exactly what challenges and serendipities 2025 will bring, either for me or for you, dear reader. Perhaps like me, you will fill this diary with flight details, work deadlines, doctor's appointments and more. I hope you make the time to care for yourself, which is one of the most radical things we can do under late capitalism. I hope you have "Nothing with coffee" or with your beverage of choice. As Jenny Odell writes in *How to Do Nothing*, "The point of doing nothing, as I define it, isn't to return to work refreshed and ready to be more productive, but rather to question what we currently perceive as productive."

Lastly, I hope these literary passages, which we have chosen with care, will provide inspiration as you go about living your days, your weeks, your year.

Milena Williamson
Managing Editor
The Irish Pages Press

On the Uses of the Imagination

In a certain sense, every historical juncture is unique and unrepeatable. Were we to choose any one of the innumerable turning-points in the human story as a stopping-place for pause and reflection, without exception we would find a complex vista unfolding before us, bristling with forms of possibility and conflict, continuity and rupture, all calibrated to the specificities of the time.

This is the nature of history; the struggle continues, as the saying goes, but so too does the effort to envision the pattern and component dynamics of the fray, with its contending velocities and complications. That envisioning, long the prerogative of poets and artists, is a matter of imaginative reach as well as observational insight, requiring that we salvage memories from the debris of the past, while intuiting the storm-signs of the emerging future – a task of perennial difficulty, unresolvable because always in-motion, which nonetheless we must attempt. Such is the writer's work. As Siegfried Sassoon discerned, in a spirit of jubilation shaded by grief, "The singing will never be done."

By assembling the diverse chorus of voices gathered here, this diary is our own attempt, as poets and editors, to respond to the challenge of twenty-first-century time. In the past two decades alone, war, famine and plague – those terrible, dark-age demons – have reappeared with fresh ferocity in the arena of human affairs, traipsing in the train of environmental despoliation and worsening the impact of catastrophic climactic events. In point of scale and intensity, indeed, the cascade of converging calamities rapidly engulfing our world has surpassed even the most apocalyptic of mediaeval and biblical premonitions, rendering dubious, for the first time in history, the likelihood of our survival as a species.

Already, the political implications of such epochal transformations are clear to see. As millions annually join the ranks of the displaced and deracinated, fleeing unliveable wastelands and collapsing states, the neoliberal myth – which could proclaim "the end of history", but only by equating unfettered globalisation with civilizational uplift and planetary progress – has bottomed out in a prolonged death-rattle of mendacities and misconceptions, still repeated by the beneficiaries of elite mis-rule and their millenarian allies, those dogged believers in the "free market". Today the very term, "freedom", has an air of pastiche or tragedy to it, one or the other, as the brash parade of neo-authoritarianism marches beneath its banner, clattering down the parliamentary corridors and dilapidated streetscapes left behind by a technocratic world order no longer trusted by its subject populations. Perhaps the well-wrought urn was hollow, all along.

Given the dire state of our circumstances, we might wonder what role remains, if any, to the engaged poet, writer, editor *or* reader. The question seems especially pertinent when the languages we share have been as depleted and degraded, as homogenised and flattened, as they have been in the years since Capitalism, that feral monolith, supposedly triumphed in its quest for global dominion, some time near the close of the 1980s.

Since then, under the combined pressures of corporate speak, clickbait journalism, AI-generated literatures, and a data-hungry "web" of online platforms awash with falsified facts and conspiratorial suspicions, the publishing industry and higher educational sector seem simply to have offered themselves up, in collusive acquiescence, to the encroaching powers. In place of a vital literary culture – conscious of collective predicaments and marked by the sweat and grist of writerly labour therein – we are given a long conveyor-belt of studious, pseudo-original "content", ethically agnostic and politically conformist, streamlined according to market needs and workshopped to conform to prevailing conventions.

The necessity for a subversive literature has never been greater. By which I mean, not works of gratuitous negation, but a body of writing capable of questioning received orthodoxies; enlightened writing, which in its form and fabric refuses the fakeries and simplifications of fascist imagining, and transcends the long sonorities, evasive and narrow, of a merely bourgeois, or indeed Anglocentric, worldview; an alert, vibrant literature, freighted and honed by the griefs and solaces of contemporary experience, and attuned to the perils and possibilities of our multitudinous present; a critical literature, searching and rich in its perceptions, stylistically supple, but grounded, also, in an awareness of the pressures of power and the intricacies of modern experience. If a universal ethical culture could some day be realised, weaving the diverse strands of the human narrative together into a faithful, legible unity, it would surely draw on the conations and recognitions furnished by such an imaginative field.

Since its foundation as a journal in 2002, and through its additional incarnations as a publisher and website in recent years, *Irish Pages* has been dedicated to seeking out and nurturing literary work of this calibre and orientation – a wide-angled, deep-rooted literature, restorative (of necessary truths) and forward-facing (in its worldly approach). To quote the editorial credo of the late Bosnian poet Vojka Smiljanić-Đikić, whose pioneering editorship of *Sarajevo Notebook*, and personal friendship, had a vital, enabling influence on one of the founders of our own project:

Everything that is new and progressive is worthy
of unreserved support and affirmation.

In an era of cultural compliance and intellectual fatigue – as the many shadows that stalk our darkening globe grow deeper – such a credo re-expresses in a positive form the task faced by serious writers, in every age: the task, as W. H. Auden's famous formulation has it, of sheltering and sustaining, in our literary labours, "an affirming flame". The authors who fill these pages are likewise exemplary. Their words spark a light for the rest of us to live by.

To begin, all we need do is read them.

Ciarán O'Rourke
Digital Editor
The Irish Pages Press

ABOUT THE JOURNAL AND THE PRESS

Irish Pages: A Journal of Contemporary Writing is a Belfast journal combining Irish, European and international perspectives. It seeks to create a novel literary space in the North adequate to the unfolding cultural potential of the new political dispensation. The magazine is cognisant of the need to reflect in its pages the various meshed levels of human relations: the regional (Ulster), the national (Ireland and Britain), the continental (Europe), and the global. It was founded in 2002 and, over the past two decades, has established itself as the island's premier literary journal, combining a large general readership with outstanding writing from Ireland and overseas.

One wider background aim is to give the journal a distinctly dissident edge, to inhabit "the space outside" the Pale of the Received – business-as-usual in all its (especially Western) forms: literary, intellectual, cultural, social, political. Thus, the journal has a particular (though hardly exclusive) commitment to work informed by "the ethical imagination". We believe that there is a huge thirst for this kind of writing – writing of "high artistic consciousness", but in the thick of the world and its dilemmas – and that it is immensely important for our increasingly complex global life. You might call it the literary equivalent of an NGO audience: all those readers for whom ethical issues count. (See our full *Credo* after the diary.)

THE IRISH PAGES PRESS
CLÓ AN MHÍL BHUÍ

Late 2018 saw the formal launch of The Irish Pages Press/Cló An Mhíl Bhuí in the sense of an annual programme of major book-publishing, under a new bilingual imprint. This was an auspicious moment for the development of a new high-profile literary press firmly rooted in Belfast and Ireland.

The Irish Pages Press will always be characterized by two essential and necessary components, flowing from the outstanding standards of *Irish Pages* in an age of media noise and publishing hyperbole: literary content of exceptional quality, and production values (always hardback) equal to any in these islands.

Currently, The Irish Pages Press is limited to poetry, essays, memoir and other forms of non-fiction (including the graphic novel form), in English, Irish and Scots.

In May 2022, The Irish Pages Press received the highly prestigious "British Book Award Small Press of the Year 2022 (Island of Ireland)." This is the first time that a press based in Northern Ireland has won any of the three relevant British Book Awards for publishers, administered by *The Bookseller* magazine in London.

In 2021-2022, The Irish Pages Press published nine titles: *Kilclief & Other Essays*, by Patricia Craig; *Ben Dorain: a conversation with a mountain*, by Garry MacKenzie; *Trump Rant*, by Chris Agee; *Gatherings of Irish Harpers 1780-1840*, by David Byers; *Phantom Gang*, by Ciarán O'Rourke; *Sappho: Songs and Poems,* by Chris Preddle; *Darkness Between Stars*, by John F. Deane and James Harpur; and *Aa Cled Wi Clouds She Cam*, by Brian Holton.

Our 2023 offering included: *Errigal*, by Cathal Ó Searcaigh; *Old Istanbul & Other Essays*, by Gerard McCarthy; *The 2024 Irish Pages Literary Diary*; and *Helen Lewis: Shadows Behind the Dance*, by Maddy Tongue.

Our 2024 offering also included: *Irish Pages: The Classic Heaney Issue*; *Genocide in Gaza* by Avi Shlaim; *Rotten London, Rotten Elsewhere: Letters to Power*, by Ahmed Olayinka Sule; *The 2025 Irish Pages Literary Diary;* and *Irish Pages*: "War in Europe" (Vol 12, No 1).

Amongst others, our 2025 offering will include: *A Week in Sarajevo & Other Essays*, by Chris Agee; *Drayhorses*, by Patricia Craig; and *Irish Pages:* "Scotland" (Vol 12, No 2).

In a major distribution agreement, Fraktura Publishing in Zagreb has chosen Irish Pages Ltd to distribute in Ireland and Britain three major award-winning works of fiction translated from the Croatian: *Invisible Woman and Other Stories*, by Slavenka Drakulić and translated by Jacob Agee; *August After Midnight*, by Luka Bekavac and translated by Ellen Elias-Bursać; and *W: A Novel* by Igor Štiks and translated by Ellen Elias-Bursać. Along with five other Fraktura titles, this is part of an EU Creative Europe project entitled "Facing Insecurities in Contemporary Europe." Fraktura is the largest literary press in the Balkans and in Southeastern Europe.

Finally, books from The Irish Pages Press have been shortlisted and longlisted for major literary prizes. *Ben Dorain: a conversation with a mountain* was shortlisted for Scotland's National Book Awards and longlisted for the Highland Book Prize; *Phantom Gang* was longlisted for the Swansea University International Dylan Thomas Prize; *Invisible Woman* was shortlisted for the European Bank of Reconstruction and Development Literature Prize 2023; and *Aa Cled Wi Clouds She Cam: 60 Lyrics frae the Chinese* (Translations in Scots and English) was nominated for the 2023 Scots Book o the Year (Scots Language Awards).

TWO POEMS BY KATHLEEN JAMIE

PIPISTRELLES

In the centre of the sheep-field
a stand of Douglas firs
hold between them, tenderly,
a tall enclosure, like a vase.

How could we have missed it
before today – just never seen
this clear, translucent vessel
tinted like citrine?

What we noticed were pipistrelles:
cinder-like, friable; flickering
the place hained by trees
till the air seemed to quicken,

and the bats were a single
edgy intelligence, testing an idea
for a new form,
which unfolded, cohered

before our eyes. The world's
mind is such interstices; cells
charging with cool dawn light;
– is that what they were telling us?

– but they vanished, suddenly,
before we'd understood,
and the trees grew in a circle,
elegant and mute.

Irish Pages: Justice (2003)

THE HILL-TRACK

But for her green
palpitating throat, they lay
inert as a stone, the male
clamped like a package
to her back. They became

as you looked, almost
beautiful, she mottled
to leafy brown, his back
marked with two stripes,
pale as over-wintered grass.

When he bucked, once,
neither even blinked:
their oval, gold-lined eyes
held to some bog-bull
imperative. The car

that would smear them
into one, belly
to belly, tongue thrust
utterly into soft brain,
approached and pressed on

oh how we press on –
the car and passengers, the slow
creatures of this earth,
the woman by the verge
with her hands cupped.

Irish Pages: Justice (2003)

2025

JANUARY

M	T	W	T	F	S	S
30	31	1	2	3	4	5
6	7	8	9	10	11	12
13	14	15	16	17	18	19
20	21	22	23	24	25	26
27	28	29	30	31	1	2
3	4	5	6	7	8	9

FEBRUARY

M	T	W	T	F	S	S
27	28	29	30	31	1	2
3	4	5	6	7	8	9
10	11	12	13	14	15	16
17	18	19	20	21	22	23
24	25	26	27	28	1	2
3	4	5	6	7	8	9

MARCH

M	T	W	T	F	S	S
24	25	26	27	28	1	2
3	4	5	6	7	8	9
10	11	12	13	14	15	16
17	18	19	20	21	22	23
24	25	26	27	28	29	30
31	1	2	3	4	5	6

APRIL

M	T	W	T	F	S	S
31	1	2	3	4	5	6
7	8	9	10	11	12	13
14	15	16	17	18	19	20
21	22	23	24	25	26	27
28	29	30	1	2	3	4
5	6	7	8	9	10	11

MAY

M	T	W	T	F	S	S
28	29	30	1	2	3	4
5	6	7	8	9	10	11
12	13	14	15	16	17	18
19	20	21	22	23	24	25
26	27	28	29	30	31	1
2	3	4	5	6	7	8

JUNE

M	T	W	T	F	S	S
26	27	28	29	30	31	1
2	3	4	5	6	7	8
9	10	11	12	13	14	15
16	17	18	19	20	21	22
23	24	25	26	27	28	29
30	1	2	3	4	5	6

JULY

M	T	W	T	F	S	S
30	1	2	3	4	5	6
7	8	9	10	11	12	13
14	15	16	17	18	19	20
21	22	23	24	25	26	27
28	29	30	31	1	2	3
4	5	6	7	8	9	10

AUGUST

M	T	W	T	F	S	S
28	29	30	31	1	2	3
4	5	6	7	8	9	10
11	12	13	14	15	16	17
18	19	20	21	22	23	24
25	26	27	28	29	30	31
1	2	3	4	5	6	7

SEPTEMBER

M	T	W	T	F	S	S
1	2	3	4	5	6	7
8	9	10	11	12	13	14
15	16	17	18	19	20	21
22	23	24	25	26	27	28
29	30	1	2	3	4	5
6	7	8	9	10	11	12

OCTOBER

M	T	W	T	F	S	S
29	30	1	2	3	4	5
6	7	8	9	10	11	12
13	14	15	16	17	18	19
20	21	22	23	24	25	26
27	28	29	30	31	1	2
3	4	5	6	7	8	9

NOVEMBER

M	T	W	T	F	S	S
27	28	29	30	31	1	2
3	4	5	6	7	8	9
10	11	12	13	14	15	16
17	18	19	20	21	22	23
24	25	26	27	28	29	30
1	2	3	4	5	6	7

DECEMBER

M	T	W	T	F	S	S
1	2	3	4	5	6	7
8	9	10	11	12	13	14
15	16	17	18	19	20	21
22	23	24	25	26	27	28
29	30	31	1	2	3	4
5	6	7	8	9	10	11

2024

JANUARY

M	T	W	T	F	S	S
1	2	3	4	5	6	7
8	9	10	11	12	13	14
15	16	17	18	19	20	21
22	23	24	25	26	27	28
29	30	31	1	2	3	4
5	6	7	8	9	10	11

FEBRUARY

M	T	W	T	F	S	S
29	30	31	1	2	3	4
5	6	7	8	9	10	11
12	13	14	15	16	17	18
19	20	21	22	23	24	25
26	27	28	29	1	2	3
4	5	6	7	8	8	10

MARCH

M	T	W	T	F	S	S
26	27	28	29	1	2	3
4	5	6	7	8	9	10
11	12	13	14	15	16	17
18	19	20	21	22	23	24
25	26	27	28	29	30	31
1	2	3	4	5	6	7

APRIL

M	T	W	T	F	S	S
1	2	3	4	5	6	7
8	9	10	11	12	13	14
15	16	17	18	19	20	21
22	23	24	25	26	27	28
29	30	1	2	3	4	5
6	7	8	9	10	11	12

MAY

M	T	W	T	F	S	S
29	30	1	2	3	4	5
6	7	8	9	10	11	12
13	14	15	16	17	18	19
20	21	22	23	24	25	26
27	28	29	30	31	1	2
3	4	5	6	7	8	9

JUNE

M	T	W	T	F	S	S
27	28	29	30	31	1	2
3	4	5	6	7	8	9
10	11	12	13	14	15	16
17	18	19	20	21	22	23
24	25	26	27	28	29	30
1	2	3	4	5	6	7

JULY

M	T	W	T	F	S	S
1	2	3	4	5	6	7
8	9	10	11	12	13	14
15	16	17	18	19	20	21
22	23	24	25	26	27	28
29	30	31	1	2	3	4
5	6	7	8	9	10	11

AUGUST

M	T	W	T	F	S	S
29	30	31	1	2	3	4
5	6	7	8	9	10	11
12	13	14	15	16	17	18
19	20	21	22	23	24	25
26	27	28	29	30	31	1
2	3	4	5	6	7	8

SEPTEMBER

M	T	W	T	F	S	S
26	27	28	29	30	31	1
2	3	4	5	6	7	8
9	10	11	12	13	14	15
16	17	18	19	20	21	22
23	24	25	26	27	28	29
30	1	2	3	4	5	6

OCTOBER

M	T	W	T	F	S	S
30	1	2	3	4	5	6
7	8	9	10	11	12	13
14	15	16	17	18	19	20
21	22	23	24	25	26	27
28	29	30	31	1	2	3
4	5	6	7	8	9	10

NOVEMBER

M	T	W	T	F	S	S
28	29	30	31	1	2	3
4	5	6	7	8	9	10
11	12	13	14	15	16	17
18	19	20	21	22	23	24
25	26	27	28	29	30	1
2	3	4	5	6	7	8

DECEMBER

M	T	W	T	F	S	S
25	26	27	28	29	30	1
2	3	4	5	6	7	8
9	10	11	12	13	14	15
16	17	18	19	20	21	22
23	24	25	26	27	28	29
30	31	1	2	3	4	5

2026

JANUARY

M	T	W	T	F	S	S
29	30	31	1	2	3	4
5	6	7	8	9	10	11
12	13	14	15	16	17	18
19	20	21	22	23	24	25
26	27	28	29	30	31	1
2	3	4	5	6	7	8

FEBRUARY

M	T	W	T	F	S	S
26	27	28	29	30	31	1
2	3	4	5	6	7	8
9	10	11	12	13	14	15
16	17	18	19	20	21	22
23	24	25	26	27	28	1
2	3	4	5	6	7	8

MARCH

M	T	W	T	F	S	S
26	27	28	29	30	31	1
2	3	4	5	6	7	8
9	10	11	12	13	14	15
16	17	18	19	20	21	22
23	24	25	26	27	28	29
30	31	1	2	3	4	5

APRIL

M	T	W	T	F	S	S
30	31	1	2	3	4	5
6	7	8	9	10	11	12
13	14	15	16	17	18	19
20	21	22	23	24	25	26
27	28	29	30	1	2	3
4	5	6	7	8	9	10

MAY

M	T	W	T	F	S	S
27	28	29	30	1	2	3
4	5	6	7	8	9	10
11	12	13	14	15	16	17
18	19	20	21	22	23	24
25	26	27	28	29	30	31
1	2	3	4	5	6	7

JUNE

M	T	W	T	F	S	S
1	2	3	4	5	6	7
8	9	10	11	12	13	14
15	16	17	18	19	20	21
22	23	24	25	26	27	28
29	30	1	2	3	4	5
6	7	8	9	10	11	12

JULY

M	T	W	T	F	S	S
29	30	1	2	3	4	5
6	7	8	9	10	11	12
13	14	15	16	17	18	19
20	21	22	23	24	25	26
27	28	29	30	31	1	2
3	4	5	6	7	8	9

AUGUST

M	T	W	T	F	S	S
27	28	29	30	31	1	2
3	4	5	6	7	8	9
10	11	12	13	14	15	16
17	18	19	20	21	22	23
24	25	26	27	28	29	30
31	1	2	3	4	5	6

SEPTEMBER

M	T	W	T	F	S	S
31	1	2	3	4	5	6
7	8	9	10	11	12	13
14	15	16	17	18	19	20
21	22	23	24	25	26	27
28	29	30	1	2	3	4
5	6	7	8	9	10	11

OCTOBER

M	T	W	T	F	S	S
28	29	30	1	2	3	4
5	6	7	8	9	10	11
12	13	14	15	16	17	18
19	20	21	22	23	24	25
26	27	28	29	30	31	1
2	3	4	5	6	7	8

NOVEMBER

M	T	W	T	F	S	S
26	27	28	29	30	31	1
2	3	4	5	6	7	8
9	10	11	12	13	14	15
16	17	18	19	20	21	22
23	24	25	26	27	28	29
30	1	2	3	4	5	6

DECEMBER

M	T	W	T	F	S	S
30	1	2	3	4	5	6
7	8	9	10	11	12	13
14	15	16	17	18	19	20
21	22	23	24	25	26	27
28	29	30	31	1	2	3
4	5	6	7	8	9	10

"We are alive at a time of sudden, necessary reappraisals, and changes of direction. History is far from over, the future struggles to find its shape. Change is happening, whether it be local, in the fracturing of the United Kingdom, or across the wide sweep of history, as revealed by the truths and hopes of the Black Lives Matter movement. It is happening on a planetary level, in the perils of climate change and species loss. Have human beings ever known such a moment?"

Kathleen Jamie, "A Time for Reappraisals", *Irish Pages: The Anthropocene* (2021)

30 Monday

31 Tuesday

1 Wednesday *New Year's Day*

2 Thursday *2nd January Holiday (Scotland)*

3 Friday

4 Saturday

5 Sunday

"We cannot do without the old, because in what is old is invested all our past, our wisdom, our memories, our sadness, our sense of realism. We cannot do without faith in the new, because in what is new is invested all our energy, our capacity for optimism, our blind biological yearning, our ability to forget – the healing ability that makes reconciliation possible."

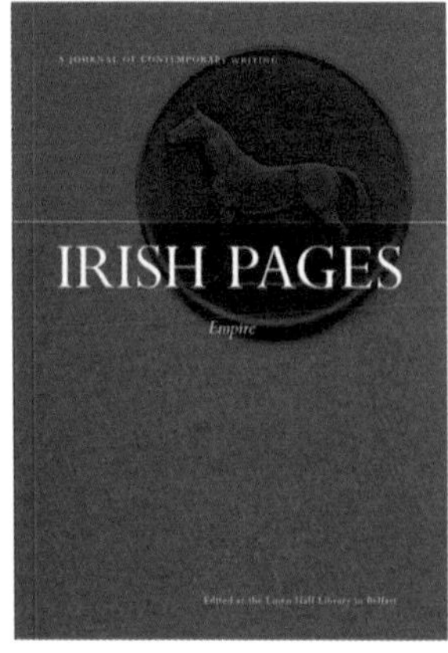

Susan Sontag, "Literature as Freedom", *Irish Pages: Empire* (2003)

6 Monday

7 Tuesday

8 Wednesday

9 Thursday

10 Friday

11 Saturday

12 Sunday

"Each one of the little fields of Árainn is so precisely defined by walls of equally individuated shapes of stone, that it offers itself as a place, as full of its own past as a room in a long-lived-in house. It probably has a name; many of the fields of Aran do. If you do not know its name it regards you mutely, asking you to find it out, or invent it. Placenames are the lingua franca of the zone of reality I have called the echosphere, the regime of echoes in which we address the habitable world and imagine that it addresses us in return ... the placename can be the incantation that turns a tract of space, a mere location, into a place ... the totality of the world's placenames constitutes humanity's full address; if we knew it we would know where we are."

Tim Robinson, "In Praise of Space", *Irish Pages: The Literary World* (2005)

13 Monday

14 Tuesday

15 Wednesday

16 Thursday

17 Friday

18 Saturday

19 Sunday

"The time has come to reconnect with the concept of slowness and slow fashion, which will require us to buy garments that are designed for long-term use. Quality of materials and construction for longevity, combined with an enthusiastic culture for fixing and repairing, can become a seductive proposition again."

Muireann Charleton, "After a Fashion", *Irish Pages: The Anthropocene* (2021)

20 Monday

21 Tuesday

22 Wednesday

23 Thursday

24 Friday

25 Saturday *Burns Night (Scotland)* 26 Sunday

"I knew nothing of Helen's background or the horrors she had experienced. She spoke briefly of the harshness of the conditions in Kochstedt, a sub-camp of Stutthof Concentration Camp near Gdansk on the Baltic coast, where, in the winter of 1944 along with others, she was forced to build an airfield for the German war effort. That day on the Dublin train her brief passing reference to the labour camp was bewildering. I recall wondering what she was talking about, what, or where did this happen. I felt the horror but had no framework, no understanding of what she might be referring to … Our bewilderment about her past life gradually lessened as on occasions she began to speak more openly about her wartime experiences. Only when she began to choreograph did it finally make sense."

Maddy Tongue,
Helen Lewis: Shadows Behind the Dance (2022)

27 Monday *International Holocaust Memorial Day*

28 Tuesday

29 Wednesday *Chinese New Year*

30 Thursday

31 Friday

1 Saturday *Imbolc (St Brigid's Day): The Beginning of Spring*

2 Sunday

"I crave some sturdy lines
slight fresh sounds
a word-poultice
that will set the soul straight
and give the body fight.

I crave the verse
that will set my soul straight."

Nuala Ní Chonchúir, "I crave some sturdy lines", (translated from the Irish of Caitlín Maude), *Irish Pages: The Home Place* (2006)

3 Monday

4 Tuesday

5 Wednesday

6 Thursday

7 Friday

8 Saturday

9 Sunday

“Wee words on reid letter paper,
Tell out hou A lou’d ye aa ma days;
The’re swan-geese in the clouds, fish in the watter –
But A’m great-hairtit wi ill-ti-scrieve feelins.

In the settin sun A hing ma lane in the westren touer,
Forenent the hingers, the ferawa hills;
A kenna whaur ma jo’s face has gane,
But the green swaws rowe eastawa, same as aye.”

—

“Little words on red letter paper,
Tell out how I loved you all my days;
There are swan-geese in the clouds, fish in the waters –
But I’m heavy-hearted with feelings impossible to write.

In the setting sun I lean alone in the western tower,
Beyond the curtain, the faraway hills;
I don’t know where my lover’s face has gone,
But the green waves roll eastward, the same as always.”

Brian Holton and Yan Shu “Ti the air o LOWN PLEISURS” / “To the air of QUIET PLEASURES”, *Aa Cled Wi Clouds She Cam* (2022)

10 Monday

11 Tuesday

12 Wednesday

13 Thursday

14 Friday *Valentine's Day*

15 Saturday

16 Sunday

"I didn't know the house, but, thus alerted, I quickly found it. Filled with curiosity, Jeff and I made our way up the lane that separated Isle O'Valla from the fields running on towards Strangford Village. We squeezed through a rusty iron gate and into the overgrown meadow where cattle sometimes grazed between the trees, and there in front of us was the house with its Georgian doorway and fanlight still intact – beautiful, spooky and utterly unreclaimable (though we didn't realise it at first). Like the House of Usher, it sported an enormous crack running the entire length of its south-facing side ... Isle O'Valla at the time had been lying derelict for more than 30 years."

Patricia Craig, "Kilclief",
Kilclief & Other Essays (2021)

17 Monday

18 Tuesday

19 Wednesday

20 Thursday

21 Friday

22 Saturday

23 Sunday

RUTH PADEL

"Writing about an animal is also writing about yourself … The one who speaks for the wild, speaks for the world."

Ruth Padel, "A Patch of Moonlight",
Irish Pages: The Anthropocene (2021)

24 Monday *Anniversary of the 2022 Invasion of Ukraine*

25 Tuesday

26 Wednesday

27 Thursday

28 Friday

1 Saturday *St David's Day (Wales)* 2 Sunday

"... the anxiety over the feminine has been the communal experience which has allowed our civilization to reveal, in a new way, the incommensurability of the individual. This incommensurability is rooted in sexual experience but nonetheless is realized through the risks that each of us is prepared to take by calling into question thought, language, one's own age and any identity which resides in them. You are a genius to the extent that you are able to challenge the socio-historical conditions of your identity."

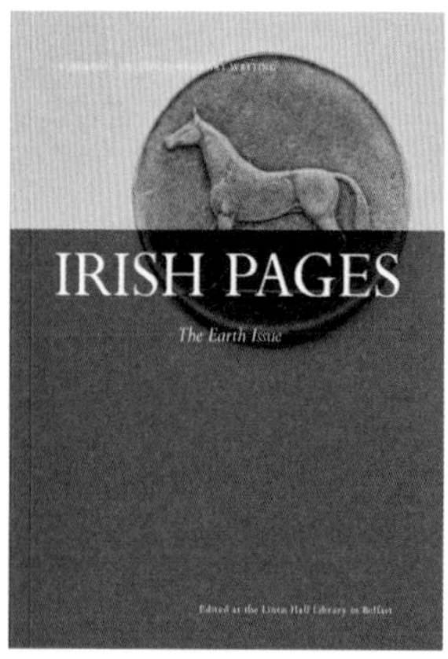

Julia Kristeva,
"Female Genius, Freedom and Culture",
Irish Pages: The Earth Issue (2004)

3 Monday *World Wildlife Day*

4 Tuesday

5 Wednesday

6 Thursday

7 Friday

8 Saturday *International Women's Day* 9 Sunday

"One thing I love most about Ireland is its almost ancient sense of self, its powerful identity, the shelves of books in Eason's exploring every nook and cranny of the country (books that people actually buy!). It's also what I like least about it. Ireland's solid brand, its seeming desire to pin its identity to the bogs, to Guinness (a multinational conglomerate!) and to bestsellers explaining how the Irish taught the world anything worth knowing, makes it so hard for us newcomers to feel like we belong. I was walking along the Old Seamus Quirke Road in the Galway rain in Wellington boots when a man in a tweed cap stopped me for some conversation. 'I see you've learned about our weather quickly!' he announced cheerfully, pointing to my sensible footwear. I was grateful for the chat – but how did he know how long I'd been here?"

Deirdre Mask, "Fitting In",
Irish Pages: Self (2011)

10 Monday

11 Tuesday

12 Wednesday

13 Thursday

14 Friday

15 Saturday

16 Sunday

"Ireland is perhaps the only country where the national talent of 'chancing your arm' has so suddenly led from stagnation to invention, where despair and corruption were turned into high enterprise. It's the only country in the world where a former head of state sued and won a libel action against a newspaper in London for being called a 'gombeen man', a unique Irish term for money-lender – a clever sort of provincial, parasitical fool."

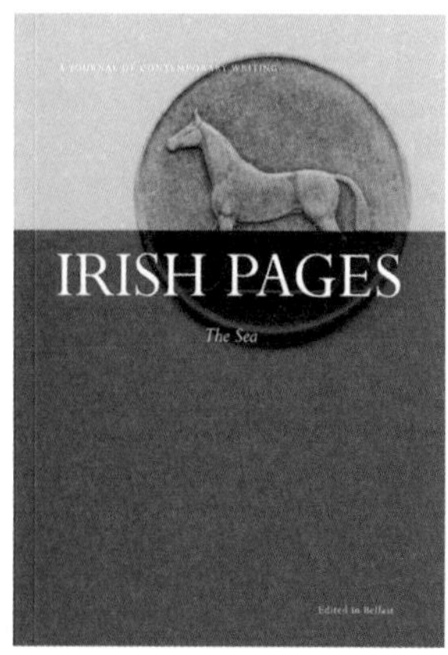

Hugo Hamilton, "The Island of Talking", *Irish Pages: The Sea* (2007)

17 Monday *St Patrick's Day (Northern Ireland/Ireland)*

18 Tuesday

19 Wednesday

20 Thursday

21 Friday

22 Saturday

23 Sunday

"Jerusalem: the mount of the ruined temple is at the centre of the question of it. That place which for millennia has been seen as the human world's opening to the transcendent. Its subterranean passions: fault-line between Christianity, Judaism and Islam: its history is at the centre of the conflict between them. The place where the One God was born. The God that was divided into three faces. The very personal God of Genesis: a figure of authority and unpredictable power, like Kafka's father. How long before there comes a generation that will not be willing to sacrifice its children?"

Gerard McCarthy, "Old Jerusalem",
Old Istanbul & Other Essays (2023)

24 Monday

25 Tuesday

26 Wednesday

27 Thursday

28 Friday

29 Saturday

30 Sunday *Eid al-Fitr*

"White-rumped, wild-headed,
holding his many-branched antlers aloft,
he has beaten the bounds of the mountain
until he wears it
like a skin.

This is pure Ben Dorain,
republic of deer."

Garry MacKenzie,
Ben Dorain: a conversation with a mountain (2020)

31 Monday

1 Tuesday

2 Wednesday

3 Thursday

4 Friday

5 Saturday

6 Sunday

"This is how hard it is for at least some of the politicians on both sides of the sectarian divide. The violence was local, intimate, not international. The killer lives, not in a distant country, but in a neighbouring village or street. Revenge is instinctive, peace-making counter-intuitive. In the *Iliad*, incensed by the fact that Hector had killed Achilles' friend Patroclus, Achilles has disrespected and defiled his victim's body by dragging it by the heels behind his chariot below the walls of Troy. Priam comes to Achilles to ask him for Hector's body, so that it can be given a proper burial. Achilles, overcome with compassion, accedes to the request, has the body washed and 'laid out in uniform' ... There is no question but that, in his encounter with the conqueror, the hero, Achilles, it is Priam who is the greater human being. This moment in the *Iliad* might even represent a genuine leap in human consciousness."

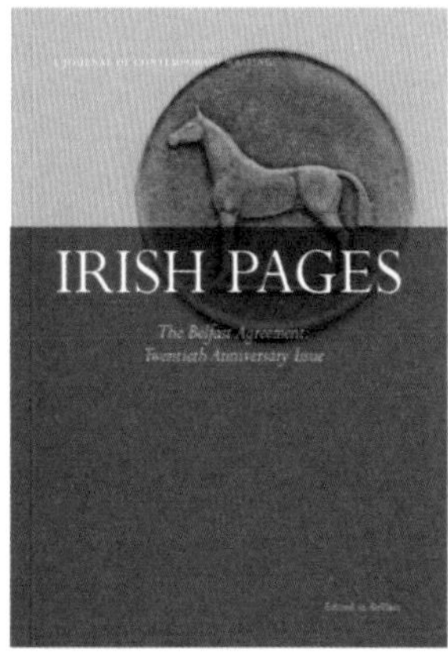

Moya Cannon,
"On the Nobility of Compromise",
Irish Pages: The Belfast Agreement (2019)

7 Monday

8 Tuesday

9 Wednesday

10 Thursday *The Belfast Agreement Anniversary*

11 Friday

12 Saturday *Passover Begins*

13 Sunday

"Supervision was done from the watchtowers that circled the camp. The towers were equipped with machine guns and at night the floodlights lit up the camp. There were also guards posted on the High Street and along the barracks at night. We normally didn't come into contact with the guards in the Street or on the towers. Of course we avoided anything that would put us in the line of fire. Even so, prisoners were shot from the towers. I remember in April 1944, when one of our group was shot on the way to the toilet …

I have strong memories of, among others, the devil in human form, 'red' Müller, who has innumerable prisoners on his conscience, and of the terrible beaters Wernicke and Hamer, of the sadist Herzog from the Shoe Kommando, Fritz Gaus and Heinz Reddehaase, of Chris the violent head of the kitchen, and last but not least Lübben the devourer of Jews and Trenkle, the head of the 'dirt camp', always drunk and always ready for abuse and I mustn't forget the inhuman head of Labour Fritz Rauh. And then the monster Kramer, the head of the camp, who permitted and encouraged all of these terrible things. These few names personify the 'hell of Bergen Belsen'.

We were ruled by the dregs of mankind."

Erich Marx, "That's How It Was: A Report on Westerbork and Bergen Belsen" (1945), *Irish Pages: Israel, Islam & the West* (2015)

14 Monday

15 Tuesday *Anniversary of the Liberation of Bergen Belsen*

16 Wednesday

17 Thursday

18 Friday *Good Friday*

19 Saturday *Easter (Holy) Saturday* 20 Sunday *Easter Sunday*

EILEEN BATTERSBY

"Writing does not have to be intellectual, but it does help if it is intelligent."

Eileen Battersby,
"On the Moral Right to Publish",
Irish Pages: Belfast in Europe (2002)

21 Monday *Easter Monday*

22 Tuesday

23 Wednesday *St George's Day (England)*

24 Thursday

25 Friday

26 Saturday

27 Sunday

JOHN BERGER

"Month by month millions leave their homelands. They leave because there is nothing there, except their everything, which does not offer enough to feed their children. Once it did. This is the poverty of the new capitalism."

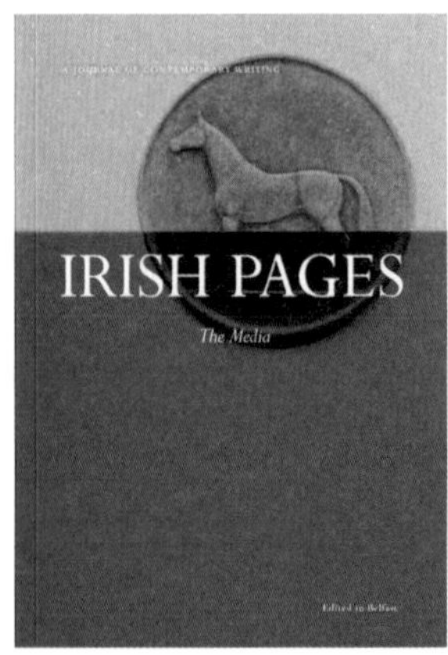

John Berger, "Ten Dispatches About Place", *Irish Pages: The Media* (2007)

28 Monday

29 Tuesday

30 Wednesday *Israeli Independence Day*

1 Thursday *Bealtaine: The Beginning of Summer*

2 Friday

3 Saturday

4 Sunday

"And then I hear it, just twice, barked into the quiet of the valley. A sharp, metallic sound. A sound out of place in nature. I stop, listening for another call, the cold grass of the verge hugging my ankles. Until this moment, I would have denied I was listening for this sound at all. But as it grates once more over fields, I remember my grandfather trying to imitate it and I know, that really, I have always been walking in expectation of hearing it in this valley again" [on the corncrake].

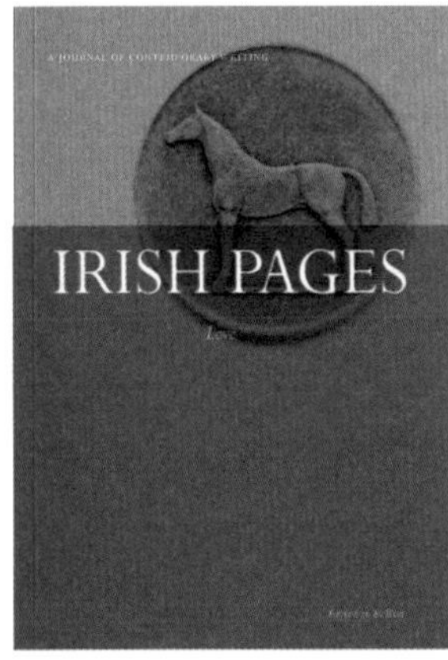

Róisín Costello, "Down to Earth", *Irish Pages: Love* (2022)

5 Monday *May Day (UK/ Ireland)*

6 Tuesday

7 Wednesday

8 Thursday

9 Friday

10 Saturday

11 Sunday

AVI SHLAIM

"My academic discipline is International Relations. In the academic literature in this field, three criteria for a rogue state are usually put forward: one, a state that habitually violates international law; two, a state that either possesses or seeks to develop weapons of mass destruction; and three, a state which resorts to terror. Terror is the use of force against civilians for political purposes. Israel meets all three criteria and therefore, in my judgement, it is now a rogue state."

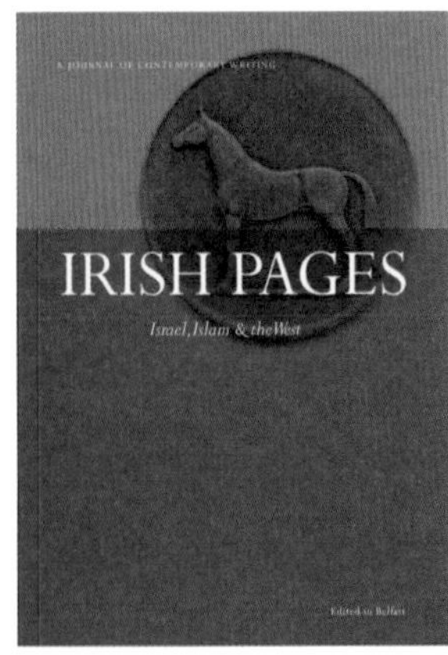

Avi Shlaim, "Israel and the Arrogance of Power", *Irish Pages: Israel, Islam & the West* (2015)

12 Monday

13 Tuesday

14 Wednesday

15 Thursday *Nakba Day*

16 Friday

17 Saturday 18 Sunday

"If the philosophical dictum of Descartes 'I think, therefore I am' represents a European individualistic ideal, the Bantu declaration '*Umuntu ngumuntu ngabantu*' represents an African communal aspiration: 'A human is human because of other humans.'

Our humanity is contingent on the humanity of our fellows. No person or group can be human alone. We rise above the animal together, or not at all. If we learned that lesson even this late in the day, we would have taken a truly millennial step forward."

Chinua Achebe, "Africa is People",
Irish Pages: The Anthropocene (2021)

19 Monday

20 Tuesday

21 Wednesday

22 Thursday

23 Friday

24 Saturday

25 Sunday *Africa Day*

"And for that brief moment, I am exactly that, a bisexual, regardless of any previous internal debate or denial or repression or confusion. As the poet C. K. Stead once said about the bird outside his window – it is what it does and it does what it is. Right now, I am stationary, smack-bang in the middle of whatever scale exists to aid in my own self-categorisation. It's as though those two poles don't exist. I am north and south, yin and yang, black and white. I am peasant and soldier, liberated, from my own battle."

Lynley Edmeades,
"Notes Towards the Geography of Desire",
Irish Pages: Sexuality (2010)

26 Monday *Spring Bank Holiday (UK)*

27 Tuesday

28 Wednesday

29 Thursday

30 Friday

31 Saturday

1 Sunday *Pride Month*

TOM PAULIN

"A truly vibrant and creative culture depends on a system of education which is not divided along class and sectarian lines … a non-sectarian education system, which will serve each and every child equally."

Tom Paulin, "The Vernacular City",
Irish Pages: Belfast in Europe (2002)

2 Monday

3 Tuesday

4 Wednesday

5 Thursday

6 Friday

7 Saturday

8 Sunday

"It was always those with almost nothing else to carry
who carried the songs
to Babylon, to the Mississippi –
hard places, both, in which to sing.
Some of these last owned less than nothing
did not own their own bodies
yet, three centuries later,
deep rhythms carried from Africa, in their hearts, their bones
pervade the world's songs.

And for those who left my own country,
girls from Downings and the Rosses
who followed herring boats up to Shetland
gutting the sea's silver as they went
or boys from Ranafast and Horn Head who took the Derry boat,
who slept over a rope in a bothy,
songs were their souls' currency,
the pure metal of their hearts,
to be exchanged for other gold,
other songs which rang out true and bright when flung down
upon the deal boards of their days."

Moya Cannon, "Carrying the Songs",
Irish Pages: Empire (2003)

9 Monday

10 Tuesday

11 Wednesday

12 Thursday

13 Friday

14 Saturday

15 Sunday

AMANDA THOMSON

"In these long summer hours of daylight, my understanding of duration alters and in old Scots Language dictionaries, I find words and phrases for the nuances of light and how a northern thread of it lingers from the end of one day to the beginning of the next, *at the head of the dim*, midsummer twilight between sunset and sunrise."

Amanda Thomson, "Biding",
Irish Pages: The Anthropocene (2021)

16 Monday

17 Tuesday

18 Wednesday

19 Thursday

20 Friday

21 Saturday *Summer Solstice* 22 Sunday

47

Eros shook
my heart like wind on a mountain attacking an oak.

48

You came, I was longing to have you,
you cooled my heart when it burned to love you.

50

The beautiful people are just appearance,
the good are beautiful at once.

Chris Preddle,
Sappho: Songs and Poems (2022)

23 Monday

24 Tuesday

25 Wednesday

26 Thursday

27 Friday

28 Saturday

29 Sunday

"The ultimate aim of society should be to make sure that people are not targeted, not harassed and not murdered because of who they are, where they come from, who they love or how they pray.

If we make that our aim – if we prioritize truth over lies, tolerance over prejudice, empathy over indifference and experts over ignoramuses – then maybe, just maybe, we can stop the greatest propaganda machine in history, we can save democracy, we can still have a place for free speech and free expression, and, most importantly, my jokes will still work."

Sacha Baron Cohen, "The Silicon Six: The Largest Propaganda Machine in History", *Irish Pages: The Anthropocene* (2021)

30 Monday

1 Tuesday

2 Wednesday

3 Thursday

4 Friday

5 Saturday

6 Sunday

"Walking that street the all-but-forgotten feeling
of eyes-on-my-back has come back.
I follow the dissident taunts on the walls

as those children once followed
the stones in the wood
and I find a flower shop about as likely

as a gingerbread house.
I buy a pot of tulips already in bud
and carry them home, hoping for red,

the colour of life, but they open white,
the colour of this arms-length stand-off
that passes itself as pure enough for a future."

Kerry Hardie, "Creggan",
Irish Pages: The Belfast Agreement: Twentieth Anniversary Issue (2018)

7 Monday

8 Tuesday

9 Wednesday

10 Thursday

11 Friday

12 Saturday

The Twelfth / Orangeman's Day (Northern Ireland)

13 Sunday

"I have no interest in introducing ranges of language or models of literature, *per se*, into Irish ... But what I do want to do above all else is to supply something, through the natural resources of the language, that hadn't been there before in poetry, in any language ... with the help of gods and demons, the unalive beings and the things that don't exist, I'll do that for whatever number of days I manage to live."

Nuala Ní Dhomhnaill, "The Ó Cadhain Lecture", *Irish Pages: The Earth Issue* (2004)

14 Monday

15 Tuesday

16 Wednesday

17 Thursday

18 Friday

19 Saturday

20 Sunday

"When an incendiary sets a match to respectability, it smoulders malodorously, but piety, like patriotism, goes off like a rocket. The jackboot was worn by the Croats themselves and used so vigorously against the schismatic Serbs that the Germans and the Italians, who had established the little state, were amazed. Pavelitch, the regicide ruler of Croatia, was himself the epitome, the personification, of the extraordinary alliance of religion and crime, which for four years made Croatia the model for all satellite states in German Europe. He was extremely devout, attending Mass every morning with his family in a private chapel built onto his house. He received expressions of devoted loyalty from the leaders of the Churches, including the Orthodox, whose murdered metropolitan had been replaced by a subservient nominee. He gave them medals and enriched their parishes with the plundered property of the schismatics, and he applied the simple creed of One Faith, One Fatherland, with a literalness that makes the heart stand still. It was an equation which had to be solved in blood. Nearly two million Orthodox were offered the alternatives of death or conversion to the faith of the majority ..."

Hubert Butler, "The Invader Wore Slippers", *Balkan Essays* (2016)

21 Monday

22 Tuesday

23 Wednesday

24 Thursday

25 Friday

26 Saturday

27 Sunday

"Tha mo nàbaid a'
  tiodhlacadh a co-ogha
is cuimhne aice air an
  latha a rugadh e;
bha e ceithir fichead 's a trì.

Thogadh e eathar,
bheireadh e bradan às a'bhàgh;
bha Gàidhlig aige air rudan
air nach biodh Beurla aig mòran;
bha cuimhne aige air iomadh
  tadhal euchdach,
air na ceudan de phuirt,
air rudan air nach bruidhneadh e …
dh'aithnicheadh e cùbhraidheachd
no fiaradh na grèine
aig àm sònraichte den bhliadhna …

Coimheadaidh sinn an ùir a' tuiteam
air ciste anns an robh cruinne-cè
nach eil ann tuilleadh."

"My neighbour is burying the cousin
she remembers being born;
he was eighty-three.

He could build a boat,
net a salmon in the bay;
knew the Gaelic for things
few know the English for;
remembered many a daring goal,
hundreds of pipe tunes,
remembered things he
  never spoke of …
would recognize a perfume
or the sun's slant
at a certain time of year …

We watch the soil shovelled in
on a coffin that contained a universe
suddenly not there."

Meg Bateman, "Tiodhlacadh"
(meaning 'Burial' in Scots Gaelic),
The Other Tongues (2013)

4 Monday *August Bank Holiday (Scotland/Ireland)*

5 Tuesday

6 Wednesday

7 Thursday

8 Friday

9 Saturday

10 Sunday

CAROLINE CLARKE

"In whatever mysterious region of the mind our memories exist, an imprint of serenity still glows in mine from that first close-up encounter with the Burren. Standing on a pavement of pale, limestone slabs on the shoreline, the restful silence is broken only by birdsong and the wash of the ocean. The smooth formations, luminous in the sunshine, are strangely compelling, giving me the urge to curl up and sleep on the warm, radiating rock. Across a glistening Galway Bay lies the hazy concertina of Connemara's Maamturk mountains and behind me the natural architecture of dry stone walls gently carves the terraced hills. At my feet delicate herb roberts and a solitary cobalt gentian draw the eye to the miniature world thriving in the grykes between the limestone clints."

Caroline Clarke, "The Burren",
Irish Pages: Self (2011)

"It hurt when I breathed in deeply. Can this be? After so many years! The smell of late summer in Dalmatia. Time passes, people come and go, even the countryside changes – whether by human hand or of its own accord, but not the smells. I stopped and shut my eyes. A traveler behind me bumped my shoulder. I turned, mechanically, to follow after the others. I brought out my French passport. The policeman said Hello in English. I answered Hello in English, too, unwilling to admit to being anything but a person holding French documents. Welcome to Croatia, he said. Thank you, I answered."

Igor Štiks,
W: A Novel (2021)

18 Monday

19 Tuesday

20 Wednesday

21 Thursday

22 Friday

23 Saturday

24 Sunday

"To feel at all: an act
of intimate dissent,

as gentle-hearted heretics
have ever felt and known.

Is this, then, our one inheritance,
the ache where voices grow?

My poem's a lifted echoing,
as if they might continue."

Ciarán O'Rourke, "The Commons",
Phantom Gang (2022)

25 Monday *Summer Bank Holiday (UK)*

26 Tuesday

27 Wednesday

28 Thursday

29 Friday

30 Saturday

31 Sunday

"Only when she rose one evening to strain the boiled pasta, only when she poured out the pasta into the strainer and the water trickled away, did she realise she was like that utensil. But unlike the strainer – which let flow on all sides – the tiny hole through which her memory had dripped was, to the naked eye, invisible and unfixable. She could hardly sense it, yet she knew it existed and felt that, slowly but steadily, she was losing herself.

Weak winter light flooded the kitchen. Who knows how much longer I will last, she reflected, conscious of the question's absurdity. This dripping, trickling, emptying was no longer separate from her, since no tiny hole can exist without its vessel. It will be easier for me when I am no longer able to remember that I can't remember, she said to herself, while placing a bowl of pasta with sauce on the table, all set for dinner."

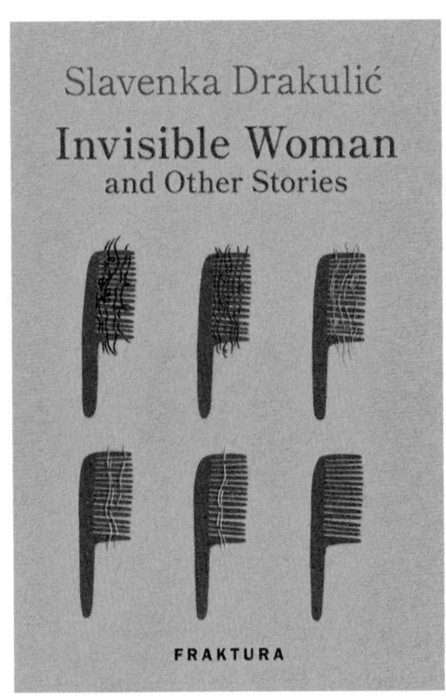

Slavenka Drakulić, "It's Nothing", *Invisible Woman & Other Stories* (2022)

1 Monday

2 Tuesday

3 Wednesday

4 Thursday

5 Friday

6 Saturday

7 Sunday

WENDELL BERRY

"Authentic peace is no more passive than war. Like war, it calls for discipline and intelligence and strength of character, though it calls also for higher principles and aims. If we are serious about peace, then we must work for it as ardently, seriously, continuously, carefully, and bravely as we have ever prepared for war."

Wendell Berry, "A Citizen's Response to the National Security Strategy of the United States", *Irish Pages: The Justice Issue* (2003)

8 Monday

9 Tuesday

10 Wednesday

11 Thursday *Anniversary of 9/11*

12 Friday

13 Saturday

14 Sunday

"The roots of the 'I' go deep; they will not be eradicated or even numbed that easily. Caught in the torque – once we're aware of being caught – we have some choice. And if it is our intimate self-awareness, our existential uniqueness, we would safeguard or seek to recover, then we might turn from the full embrace of our networks and reconnect to the one-on-one circuitry of art. Art serves the soul not least by demanding and creating attention. This same attention in its early stages allows us to winnow the meaningful signal from the distracting noise, and ultimately rejuvenates the connection of self to the world."

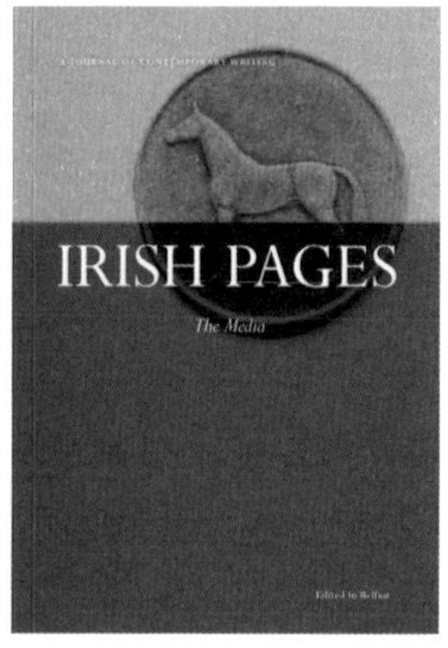

Sven Birkerts, "The Drowning Signal: Self in the Information Age", *Irish Pages: The Media* (2007)

15 Monday

16 Tuesday

17 Wednesday

18 Thursday

19 Friday

20 Saturday

21 Sunday

TOM MAC INTYRE

"Listen for a silence. That silence. And it arrives, brimming embrace. Comes a moment you begin to long for it. Court it. Head bowed, name it home."

Tom Mac Intyre, "Memoirs", *Irish Pages: Memory* (2013)

22 Monday *Rosh Hashanah (Jewish New Year)*

23 Tuesday

24 Wednesday

25 Thursday

26 Friday

27 Saturday

28 Sunday

ANNE DEVLIN

"And there is the nub: in '68 we did not want the national history, the unfinished business of the civil war. We wanted to live in '68. We wanted to live in our own time. This is what gave my generation identity and direction."

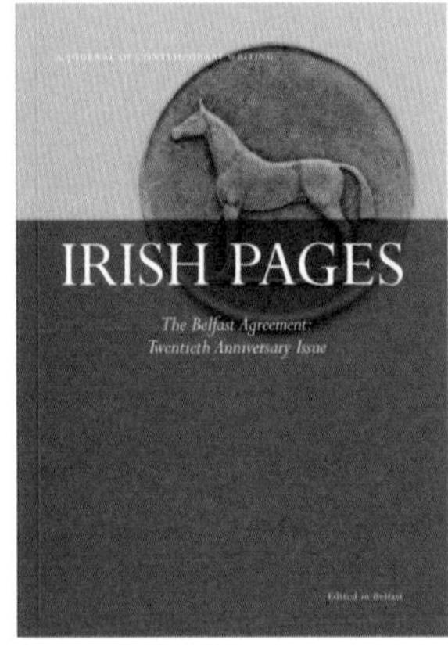

Anne Devlin, "Responsibility for the Dead",
Irish Pages: The Belfast Agreement (2019)

29 Monday

30 Tuesday

1 Wednesday *Yom Kippur (Day of Atonement)*

2 Thursday

3 Friday

4 Saturday

5 Sunday *Anniversary of Civil Rights March in Derry, 1968*

"... Cinema and art aren't the icing on the cake, they are the cake. Movies make us feel alive, connected. Cinema makes moments seem more than they were, as big as the sphinx, as available for inspection, as gnomic, as here and not here as life, as sensuous and intoxicating."

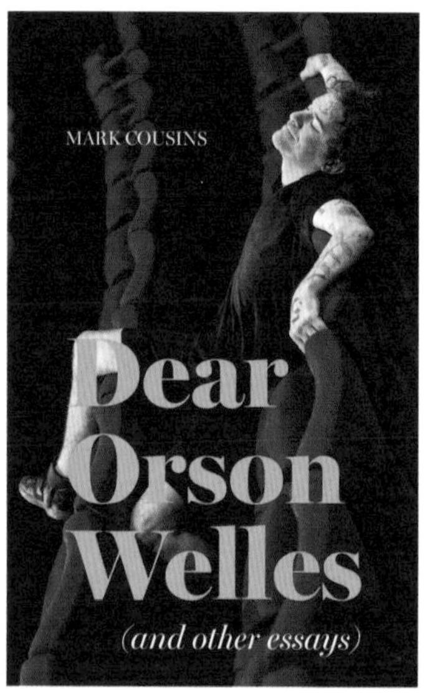

Mark Cousins,
Dear Orson Welles & Other Essays (2024)

6 Monday

7 Tuesday

8 Wednesday

9 Thursday

10 Friday

11 Saturday

12 Sunday

"Now, dialogue may seem like an overused term, and a facile panacea; but in fact, authentic dialogue is anything but easy. It needs empathy and it needs courage. It cannot proceed from the position either of putative superiority, or self-effacement. To condescend to our interlocutors in such encounters is of course to diminish and humiliate them; but to defer to others automatically because we perceive them as vulnerable, or less privileged, or as 'our victims' – is to assume that they are divested of agency and incapable of responsibility. From the minority side, such dialogue also requires an effort of openness and the courage to step outside the rules of the tribe. If we perceive our interlocutors merely as representatives of power, or as incapable of real understanding or change, we are guilty of prejudice too. And again, I say 'we', because I have been on that side of the equation as well. Equality, it seems to me, is not only an economic, but an ethical achievement."

Eva Hoffman, "On Internal Others",
Irish Pages: Criticism (2018)

13 Monday

14 Tuesday

15 Wednesday

16 Thursday

17 Friday

18 Saturday

19 Sunday

"The emotional instability around anger, betrayal and pain brings us close to chaos. But a return to 'normality' would mean an odd kind of loss. Somewhere there is an awareness in us that we are living on a different plane, and somewhere we also crave the purity and intensity of this plane—as those whose lungs are used to high clean air crave relief from the smog and fumes of a city. On this other level it is possible to be alone with your dead and to feel their presence. This is hard to let go of, though it must be accomplished. It is the only thing that will bring about the release of the dead. To dwell there too long is not our purpose in life. Somehow we must find the grace to accept the living."

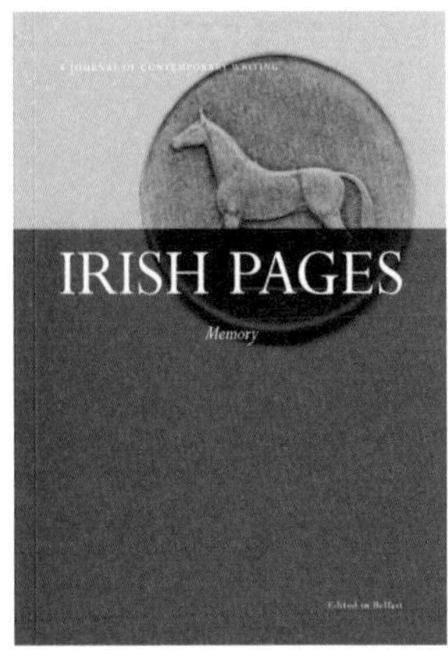

Kerry Hardie, "Aftermath",
Irish Pages: Memory (2013)

20 Monday

21 Tuesday

22 Wednesday

23 Thursday

24 Friday

25 Saturday

26 Sunday

"As long ago as the first industrial revolution in Britain the end of poetry was predicted, as by Thomas Carlyle. The prediction was proved wrong, both because the squalor brought in by that revolution created a need to escape from it – the Romantic Movement – and because an expanding readership, even for poetry, could be served by the mass production of written texts. The reversal of that development may now look like the end of a whole culture, the literate one, in which literacy was bound up with an awareness of the past – a selected past, therefore 'elitist' in the terminology of those who confuse class resentments with considerations of quality. This reversal is still resisted here and there, by dwindling minorities, but other threats of environmental, economic and political disasters detract again and again from the urgency of the resistance, now that it is not the continuity of one culture, one civilisation, but of life on our planet that is in question. Any prediction about the future of poetry would rest on the complacent assumption that the larger destruction can still be averted."

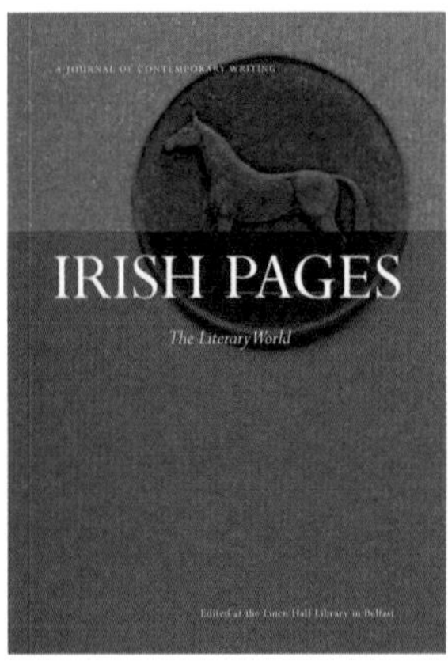

Michael Hamburger,
"Afterthoughts on the Mug's Game",
Irish Pages: The Literary World (2005)

27 Monday *October Bank Holiday (Ireland)*

28 Tuesday

29 Wednesday

30 Thursday

31 Friday *Samhain (Hallowe'en): The Beginning of Winter*

1 Saturday

2 Sunday

"In the multitude of lessons that fascism involuntarily left for us in its legacy, most valuable is the moral imperative that we watch the homeland with pitiless skepticism. Without this skepticism the survival of democracy, and thus of civilisation, is not possible. That such a bloody message was needed at all is shameful."

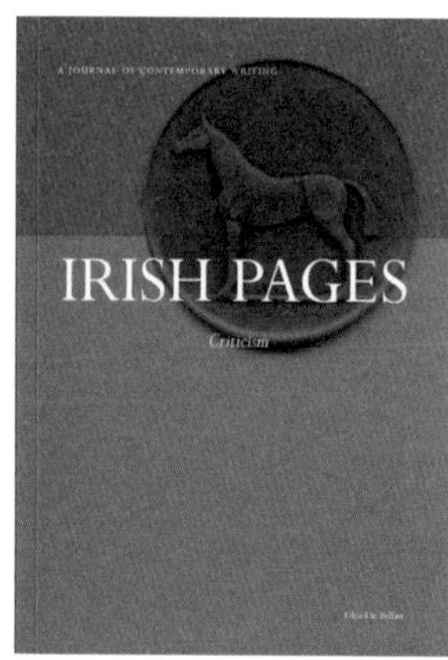

Vuk Perišić, "The World as Weimar",
Irish Pages: Criticism (2018)

3 Monday

4 Tuesday

5 Wednesday

6 Thursday

7 Friday

8 Saturday

9 Sunday *Remembrance Sunday (UK)*

“Trump Is Mob Culture
Trump Likes Interpersonal Power
Trump Makes Enemies
Trump Mocks
Trump Is New York
Trump Loves the East
Trump Hates Change
Trump Is a Grifter
Trump Is Impermeable
Trump Never Laughs”

Chris Agee,
Trump Rant (2020)

10 Monday

11 Tuesday

12 Wednesday

13 Thursday

14 Friday

15 Saturday

16 Sunday

"Teach tréigthe roimhe anocht.
Ar an tairseach, faoi lom na gealaí, nocht,
scáile an tseanchrainn a chuir sé blianta ó shin."

"He's back tonight to a deserted house.
On the doorstep, under a brilliant moon, a stark
shadow: the tree he planted years ago is an old tree."

(translated by Seamus Heaney)

Cathal Ó Searcaigh,
"Pilleadh an Deoraí" / "Exile's Return",
Crann na Teanga / The Language Tree (2018)

17 Monday

18 Tuesday

19 Wednesday

20 Thursday

21 Friday

22 Saturday

23 Sunday

"We humans are meaning-making, and meaning-seeking creatures. We do not live by economic interests alone; and in order to understand why democracy matters, and why it deserves our allegiance, we need a discourse not only of economics, but of meanings … One of our deepest grown-up desires is for solidarity – for living in a shared social space with fellow human beings whom we can respect and understand, and to whom we can extend basic trust, if not always agreement."

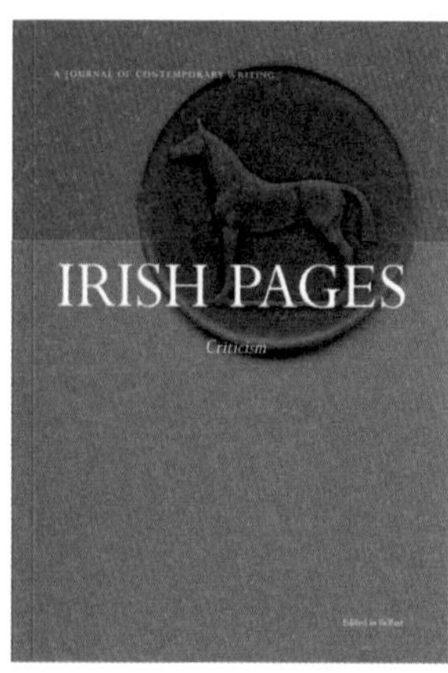

Eva Hoffman, "On Internal Others",
Irish Pages: Criticism (2018)

24 Monday

25 Tuesday

26 Wednesday

27 Thursday *Thanksgiving (USA)*

28 Friday

29 Saturday

30 Sunday *St Andrew's Day (Scotland)*

"How can one assume a neutrality when addressing the cultural air we breathe? How can one see one's heritage unless one steps outside it into that space we share in common with all heritages: the world that none of us can step outside – until the final voyage to the final boundary, from which no voyager returns?"

Gerard McCarthy,
"Home from Andalucia",
Old Istanbul & Other Essays (2023)

1 Monday *St Andrew's Day: Substitute Holiday (Scotland)*

2 Tuesday

3 Wednesday

4 Thursday

5 Friday

6 Saturday

7 Sunday

"The beauty of art, including poetry, is that it transcends all tribalism and division, or should do; the melting pot of the Imagination has no limit to it, no barriers and invites anything and everything into its warm embrace in order for the strange alchemy of creation to work its magic."

James Harpur, "Poetry, God and the Imagination: A Dialogue", *Darkness Between Stars* (2022)

8 Monday

9 Tuesday

10 Wednesday

11 Thursday

12 Friday

13 Saturday

14 Sunday *Beginning of Chanukah*

"Is it any wonder that Wittgenstein went to Connemara, the furthest point west, to look back and see something clearly in what he called Europe's 'last pool of darkness'? ... If I want to know what is true in life, is it any wonder that I need the absolute darkness to see the light so clearly?"

Leslie Van Gelder, "On Absolute Darkness", *Irish Pages: Inheritance* (2014)

15 Monday

16 Tuesday

17 Wednesday

18 Thursday

19 Friday

20 Saturday

21 Sunday *Winter Solstice*

"Sometimes when you walk down to the red gate
hearing the scrape-music of your shoes across gravel,
a yellow moon will lift over the hill;
you swing the gate shut and lean on the topmost bar
as if something has been accomplished in the world;
a night wind mistles through the poplar leaves
and all the noise of the universe stills
to an oboe hum, the given note of a perfect
music; there is a vast sky wholly dedicated
to the stars and you know, with certainty,
that all the dead are out, up there, in one
holiday flotilla, and that they celebrate
the fact of a red gate and a yellow moon
that tunes their instruments with you to the symphony."

John F. Deane, "Canticle",
Darkness Between Stars (2022)

22 Monday

23 Tuesday

24 Wednesday *Christmas Eve*

25 Thursday *Christmas Day*

26 Friday *Boxing Day (UK), St Stephen's Day (Ireland) & Beginning of Kwanzaa*

27 Saturday

28 Sunday

"When I first saw Seamus at that poetry reading in Cambridge, I saw him as a justly celebrated author of a number of poems that had stirred me. My excitement was also, it's true, a kind of confusion. Confusion – and this is maybe a bit exaggerated – between my experience of the poems, which are felt to be somehow outside ordinary time, and the slightly rumpled physical immediacy of their maker. But I remind myself – and believe, if only to preserve my self-esteem – that, confusion or no, the primary attraction was finally less the fact of his public notoriety and more that he was the man who had written these many great poems. As soon as the meeting happened, the acquaintance – and the eventual friendship, of course – the distinction grew blurred. But on the far side of the complex assessment of motives, intents and incentives, I believe things were clear enough. After all, here was the basis of the mattering of literature."

Sven Birkerts, "Seamus Heaney: Notes on Fame and Friendship", *Irish Pages: The Classic Heaney Issue* (2023)

29 Monday

30 Tuesday

31 Wednesday *New Year's Eve / Hogmanay*

1 Thursday *New Year's Day*

2 Friday *2nd January Holiday (Scotland)*

3 Saturday

4 Sunday

TWO MICROPOEMS BY CHRIS AGEE

There it is

splendiferous London
lit bridges
girded over
the serpentine Thames
jewelled honeycomb
of hope
and joys and love
misery and power
this century's
high plateau
vulnerable before
the plagues and epidemics
that will surely come

Flight from Vienna
16 February 2013

From *Blue Sandbar Moon* (The Irish Pages Press, 2018)

The poppies

are proliferating
in June
on the communal path
through our land
back towards
old Miko
and Austria-Hungary
on the map of the subtle hues
on the hall wall
the seven states
of his span
the eight wars
of a Balkan century

or forwards towards
the sea-dead
off Roman Libya
or the Aegean's
inflatable coracles
or corpses
heading
to the end
of the nation
state
in a new republic
of equal
lives

Ireland-Croatia
June-July 2016

From *Blue Sandbar Moon* (The Irish Pages Press, 2018)

OUR CREDO

2003 – 2025

Appearing twice a year, *Irish Pages* is a Belfast journal combining Irish, European and international perspectives. It seeks to create a novel literary space, North and South, adequate to the unfolding cultural potential of the island's new political dispensation. The magazine is cognisant of the need to reflect in its pages the various meshed levels of human relations: the regional (Ulster), the national (Ireland and Britain), the continental (the whole of Europe), and the global.

Since its full-scale launch in 2003, *Irish Pages* has established itself as the island's premier literary journal, combining a large general readership with outstanding writing from Ireland and overseas. With a print-run now standing at 3,000, the journal is also, increasingly, read outside Ireland and Britain. Widely considered the Irish equivalent of *Granta* in England, or *The Paris Review* in the United States, it offers an unrivalled window on the literary and cultural life of these islands – and further afield.

Each issue assembles a carefully edited mix of English, Irish and Scots, prose and poetry, fiction and non-fiction, style and subject-matter, in an overall fit aimed at a wide range of reading tastes. The cover theme suggests some of the content, and emerges from the editorial process – the blend of what is selected from submissions, and what is sought or commissioned.

In addition, *Irish Pages* includes a number of regular or occasional features: *The View from the Lagan*, an editorial commenting on cultural or political issues from Ireland and overseas; *From the Irish Archive*, an extract of writing from a non-contemporary Irish writer, or on a noncontemporary Irish theme; *In Other Words*, a selection of translated work from a particular country; and *The Publishing Scene*, a piece taking a critical look at some aspect of the literary world in Ireland, Britain or the United States. Each issue also contains an outstanding portfolio of colour or black-and-white photography from a leading photographer; an article on Belfast or Northern Ireland; work from at least one emergent or new writer; writing on the natural world; and a major essay of literary distinction on an ethical, historical, religious, social or scientific topic. There are *no* standard reviews or narrowly scholarly articles: the journal is most definitely *not* an academic publication. Irish Language and Scots writing are published in the original, often with English translations or glosses.

Although *Irish Pages* is mainly a prose journal, poetry is, of course, a major component of the journal's mix of genres. On average, about a third of contributors, and about a fifth of each issue is given over to poetry, in both Irish and English, and including translations from other languages. Several issues have additionally carried a substantial essay on the poetic art by a noted practitioner. This distinct but circumscribed space for poetry reflects the view of the poet-editors that in the context of a general readership journal such as ours, a lean selection of poetry is likely to be read more attentively within the overall mix.

The only criteria for inclusion in the journal are the distinction of the writing and the integrity of the individual voice. There are no favoured styles, themes, schools, publishers, critical hierarchies, ethnicities and so on. Equal attention will be given to established, emergent *and* new writers.

Some Different Things about Irish Pages

There are, in fact, very few literary journals that avoid reviews and cognate varieties of academic criticism (although we do publish the occasional literary "essay-review", or critical essay). Why attempt what the *The Times Literary Supplement* or *London Review of Books* will always do better? *Irish Pages* represents a new paradigm focussing entirely on the reading of "primary" writing, rather than its critical or "secondary" mediation.

We wish the journal to be read widely and each issue's careful mix of genres and styles is essential to the magazine's appeal outside the ghetto of the literati. There is an especial commitment – uniquely for Ireland and perhaps Britain, at least in a literary journal – to nature/ecological writing as well as creative non-fiction/the essay. And although each issue will carry at least one and often two pieces of fiction, part of the thinking behind this mix is to provide an antidote or an alternative to the enormous critical and commercial attention that is given to the various genres of fiction, at the expense clearly of other genres, whose historical/ethical/social value is surely no less.

Writing in Irish (and Scots Gaelic on occasion) is integral to the editorial mix. To date we have published poetry, drama, fiction and criticism in Irish; we have also published first translations *as Gaeilge* of a clutch of important essays by major Irish-language writers. We attempt to place the two languages in seamless juxtaposition, to suggest their parity in any definition of the "Irish" in *Irish Pages*. Outside the Irish language world *per se*, the publishing of Irish-language writing in journals is often tinged with tokenism; we pursue a much more active bilingualism.

One wider background aim is to give the journal a distinctly dissident edge, to inhabit "the space outside" the Pale of the Received – business-as-usual in all its (especially Western) forms: literary, intellectual, cultural, social, political. Thus, the journal has a particular (though hardly exclusive) commitment to work informed by "the ethical imagination". We believe that there is a huge thirst for this kind of writing – writing of "high artistic consciousness", but in the thick of the world and its dilemmas – and that it is immensely important for our increasingly complex global life. You might call it the literary equivalent of an NGO audience: all those readers for whom ethical issues count.

The Editor

BOOKS PUBLISHED BY THE IRISH PAGES PRESS

Genocide in Gaza: Israel's Long War On Palestine by Avi Shlaim (2024)
Dear Orson Welles & Other Essays by Mark Cousins (2024)
Irish Pages: The Classic Heaney Issue edited by Chris Agee
(Commemorative Reprint, 2023: first published 2014)
Errigal: Sacred Mountain by Cathal Ó Searcaigh (2023)
Old Istanbul & Other Essays by Gerard McCarthy (2023)
Helen Lewis: Shadows Behind the Dance by Maddy Tongue (2022)
Aa Cled Wi Clouds She Cam: 60 Lyrics frae the Chinese
(Translations in Scots and English) by Brian Holton (2022)
Phantom Gang by Ciarán O'Rourke (2022)
Sappho: Songs and Poems by Chris Preddle (2022)
Darkness Between Stars by John F. Deane and James Harpur (2022)
Gatherings of Irish Harpers 1780 – 1840 by David Byers (2022)
Trump Rant by Chris Agee (2021)
Kilclief & Other Essays by Patricia Craig (2021)
Ben Dorain: a conversation with a mountain by Garry MacKenzie (2021)
The Buried Breath by Ciarán O'Rourke (2018)
Crann na Teanga / The Language Tree by Cathal Ó Searcaigh (2018)
Blue Sandbar Moon by Chris Agee (2018)
Balkan Essays by Hubert Butler (2016)
The Other Tongues edited by Chris Agee et al. (2013)
New Voices: Contemporary Poetry from the United States edited by H.L. Hix (2008)
Unfinished Ireland: Essays on Hubert Butler edited by Chris Agee (2002)

BOOKS DISTRIBUTED BY THE IRISH PAGES PRESS

Published by Fraktura Publishing, Zagreb, Croatia

Cloud the Color of Skin by Nebojša Lujanović (2024)
Unterstadt – A Novel by Ivana Šojat (2024)
The Story of a Man Who Collapsed Into His Notebook by Ivana Sajko (2024)
Theory of Sorrow by Slavenka Drakulić (2023)
Invisible Woman and Other Stories by Slavenka Drakulić (2022)
Daddy Issues by Dino Pešut (2022)
August After Midnight by Luka Bekavac (2022)
W: A Novel by Igor Štiks (2021)

A NOTE ON THE DIARY TEXTS

All the texts used in *The 2025 Irish Pages Literary Diary* are extracts from either *Irish Pages: A Journal of Contemporary Writing*, or titles published or distributed by The Irish Pages Press. All of these publications can be ordered at our website: www.irishpages.org, which includes a full list of the journal issues since 2002.

NOTES

NOTES

NOTES

NOTES

NOTES

Outstanding Writing from Ireland and Overseas

THE IRISH PAGES PRESS
CLÓ AN MHÍL BHUÍ

On Receiving

"THE BRITISH BOOK AWARD SMALL PRESS OF THE YEAR 2022 (ISLAND OF IRELAND)":

"Congratulations for your long, honorable, and original service to writers and writing!"

Helen Vendler
(1933-2024)

Scholar, essayist and critic

Porter University Professor Emerita, Harvard University